How to Win at
CARD
GAMES

Belinda Levez

TEACH YOURSELF BOOKS

Long-renowned as the authoritative source for self-guided learning – with more than 30 million copies sold worldwide – the *Teach Yourself* series includes over 200 titles in the fields of languages, crafts, hobbies, sports, and other leisure activities.

Library of Congress Catalog Card Number: 96-69674

First published in UK 1997 by Hodder Headline Plc, 338 Euston Road, London NW1 3BH

Catalogue entry for this title is available from the British Library.

First published in US 1997 by NTC Publishing Group
An imprint of NTC/Contemporary Publishing Company
4255 West Touhy Avenue, Lincolnwood (Chicago), Illinois 60646 – 1975 U.S.A.

The 'Teach Yourself' name and logo are registered trade marks of Hodder & Stoughton Ltd in the UK.

Copyright © 1997 Belinda Levez

Typeset by Transet Limited, Coventry, England.
Printed in England by Cox & Wyman Ltd, Reading, Berkshire.

Impression number	10	9	8	7	6	5	4	3
Year			2000	1999	1998	1997		

CONTENTS

INTRODUCTION

Many people play card games with varying degrees of success. Some win money but a lot lose. Many of the losses could be avoided and are often due to a lack of knowledge about the games and poor methods of play. Too many people rely on luck instead of skill.

Some games are simply not worth playing because they give poor returns to the player. Others that give a fairer chance may incorporate some bets that are not worth bothering with. This book aims to teach you how profitable the various games are so that you can make an informed choice about those that are worth playing. The rules are also described so that you can learn how to play properly. You will be taught how to get better value for money, as well as methods of play that maximise winnings whilst keeping losses to a minimum. Lots of illustrated examples are given to make the understanding of the games easier.

The issues which you need to consider when gambling are covered. Advice is given on where to gamble and the dangers involved with illegal gambling and private games are highlighted. You are also shown how to avoid the tricks that casinos use to make you spend more money.

By the end of the course you will be a more informed gambler with a better understanding of the subject. With plenty of practice you will also become a more skilful player and hopefully a winner instead of a loser. Good luck!

1
BEFORE YOU BET

There are lots of issues that you need to consider before you bet. You may already know some gamblers, and they have probably recounted stories of their big wins. It is highly unlikely, however, that they have told you how much money they have lost! A lot of gamblers will tell you that they always break even. If this is true, why do casinos make such huge profits? No matter what other gamblers tell you, do not assume that it is easy to win.

Gambling is risky – you can easily lose. When gamblers start losing there is a tendency to try to recoup losses by betting more heavily. This can lead to financial ruin. Gambling can also become addictive, so if you find that your betting is getting out of control, you should contact one of the Gamblers Anonymous organisations. Details are given on page 68. You can guard against this situation arising by ensuring that you take a sensible approach of gambling.

Set a budget

Before you place any bets, you need to be certain that you do not lose more than you can afford. Take a pen and paper and work out a financial budget. Calculate all your household and living costs. Make sure that you include all expenses. Find out what your disposable income is and then decide how much of it you can comfortably afford to lose. The amount that you have calculated is your budget for gambling.

Be sure to stick to your budget. Never be tempted to make additional bets from, for example, your rent money. If you keep to your budget then you can gamble with the knowledge that no matter how much you lose you will not go bankrupt.

When you gamble take only your stake money and enough for your expenses (fare home, drinks, meals, etc). Leave all cheque books and cash cards at home. If you can't get your hands on more money, you can't spend it. Don't be tempted to borrow money from friends and decline all offers of credit. If you run out of money, either go home or just spectate.

If you don't want to carry large amounts of cash, open a separate bank account for your gambling money and take with you only the cheque book and cards relating to that account when you gamble.

Find your game

One of the main considerations when deciding what game to play is how involved you want to be. With games like poker and blackjack you need to make lots of decisions. They require skill, knowledge and complete concentration to make the best choice. With games like punto banco and baccara-chemin de fer there are rules that determine what happens next, you do not need to make any choices. You just need to decide how much to bet.

Be aware of the rules

Before you go to a casino, learn how to play the games. This may seem like common sense advice but so many people go along and gamble with little or no knowledge about the games they are playing. Losing all your money can prove an expensive lesson.

Appreciate your chances of winning

Have a thorough understanding of the odds against winning. The casino makes a profit by paying out winnings at lower than the true odds. The amount the casino deducts varies with different establishments and games. Before you play find out how much profit the casino is taking. If their advantage is too great it may not be worthwhile playing.

Keep records of your gambling

Try to keep accurate records of your betting. Also write down the reasons why you win or lose. Periodically analyse your results. By keeping records you will be in a much better position to assess your betting strategy and to make changes if it is not effective.

British casinos

Great Britain has over 120 legal casinos. They tend to be found in large towns and cities and in tourist areas. There are over twenty in London. They are strictly controlled by the Gaming Board who issue licences for premises and casino staff. Checks are carried out to ensure that no gaming personnel or casino owners have criminal records. Card games played include blackjack, punto banco and poker. Daily opening hours are from 2.00 pm to 4.00 am.

United States casinos

Gaming is legal in most of the United States (only nine states do not have casinos). Casinos are built on a massive scale and often incorporate theme parks. There is a wide choice of card games including blackjack, punto banco, red dog and poker. Many casinos are open twenty-four hours a day.

Selecting a casino

The amount you have budgeted for will largely determine the sort of club you frequent. The minimum stakes for betting can vary quite considerably in different casinos. Generally the more upmarket the club, the higher the stakes will be.

You should consider how many chips of the minimum stake your budget will purchase and how long they will last. The low stake tables are always the most crowded in the casino. The higher stake tables are generally quieter. Most casinos also have private rooms (salon privé). These are usually for players betting high stakes.

Dress code

Many casinos impose dress codes, particularly the most upmarket establishments, and you may be refused admittance if you do not meet the required standard.

Tricks casinos use to get you to spend more money

Casinos employ many subtle methods to get as much money from you as possible. By using car jockeys they can ensure you spend more time in the casino. Why make you spend fifteen minutes finding a parking space when you could spend that time gambling? It is also common practice not to have any clocks or exterior windows in the gaming rooms. This ensures that you lose track of time.

In casinos you exchange your money for plastic chips. This takes away the associations you have with money. When you see a bank note, you appreciate its value and how long it would take you to earn it. Chips resemble coins which have very little value.

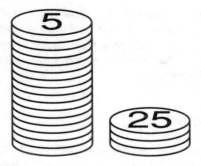

Figure 1.1 Casino chips

When you go to a casino try not to change all of your money into chips. Exchange it in small amounts. If you have to keep going to your wallet, you will have a better appreciation of how much money you are spending.

Free refreshments are often supplied to keep you in the casino. The longer you spend there the more money you are likely to gamble. Try to avoid alcohol. It affects your ability to concentrate and you are more likely to make mistakes. It also lowers your inhibitions so you are less likely to care if you are losing.

Figure 1.2 Avoid alcohol whilst playing

2
CHEATING

Whatever game you choose to play, one of the most important considerations is that you have a fair chance of winning. The best way to guarantee this is to gamble only in legal casinos.

Although illegal casinos and private games may offer some concessions that appear to work in the player's favour, such as tax-free betting and better payout odds, it is far too easy for the house to cheat. There are lots of ways in which gamblers can be duped.

As well as cheating, illegal casinos may offer you unlimited credit. This can make it very easy for you to go over budget. An illegal casino's methods for recouping the money you owe may also be highly suspect.

Card games are particularly vulnerable to cheating. If you play in private games, you should be aware of the many methods of cheating so that you can ensure that you are not conned.

Methods of cheating

Substituting a cold deck

By creating a distraction a cold deck can be substituted for the one in play. A cold deck is a pack of cards arranged in a pre-set order. A player knowing the order of the cards can ensure that he wins.

Betting light

One of the easiest ways to cheat is for players to not fully contribute to the pot. If there are a lot of chips already in the pot, it is not always obvious how many chips a particular player is adding. You may see him pick up the required number of chips, but it is very easy to just drop a few into the pot and palm the rest. Everyone's attention then switches to the next player and the one who palmed the chips is able to discreetly put them back on the table with his own chips.

Alternatively a cheat may bet so quickly that you do not see what chips he picks up. The only indication that you get of a bet being made is the clinking of the chips as more are added.

Marked cards

In games like poker it is advantageous for gamblers to know what cards the other players are holding. Anyone with this knowledge is able to bet only when he knows he has a winning hand.

The easiest way to accomplish this is to mark the backs of the cards in such a way so that they can be 'read' by the cheat. The designs on the backs of cards are intricate patterns. It is possible to add shading, small dots or to slightly thicken lines. These changes will not be noticed by the other players unless the cards are carefully scrutinised.

Even if someone produces a sealed pack of cards, they may still be marked. It is a relatively simple task to mark the cards and reseal them in their original packing. Professionally marked cards can also be purchased. The designs may be identical but certain cards may have a slightly thicker border on one side.

Marks are harder to spot on cards with pictorial designs on their backs. It is better to play with cards that have uniform patterns on their backs. This style of card is used in casinos as any marks are easier to spot.

Before you begin playing you should carefully study the cards. Pay particular attention to the corners. Marks are placed here so that they can be seen when players are holding their cards. Compare the high cards to the low cards. Often only the high cards will be marked.

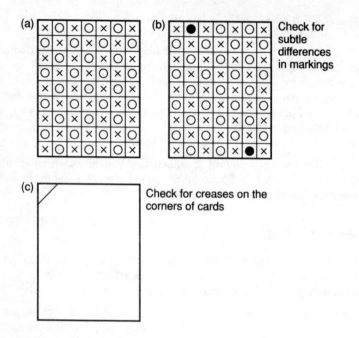

Figure 2.1 Cheating using marked cards

Cards should also be checked during the course of play as they can become marked either intentionally or accidentally. Most commonly corners of cards can be bent to make creases visible. If any marks are found use a new pack of cards.

Technicians

Dealers can cheat in lots of ways. Someone who is skilled at manipulating the cards is called a technician. It is easy to look at the bottom card whilst shuffling. With practice it is possible to position desired cards at the bottom of the pack. The dealer can then deal his hand from the bottom of the deck and the other player's hands from the top.

Another method is to spot a good card whilst shuffling and to place it on the top of the deck. The dealer saves this card for himself and deals from the second card down to the other players.

A player can also use a spiked ring to make an indentation in the cards. When it is his turn to deal, he simply has to feel the cards to identify the best ones. He can either save them for himself using one of the techniques already described or simply keep track of which player receives them.

Cutting the cards

To combat cheating by the dealer it is common practice for one of the players to cut the cards. However, the dealer can overcome the problem of the cards being cut by bending one card in the middle so that it is slightly curved. The cards will tend to be cut at the curved card. You can try this yourself with a pack of cards. You easily grip the curved card but the ones below it slip through your fingers. A dealer cannot guarantee that it will work every time but on the occasions that it does, he is guaranteed of a win.

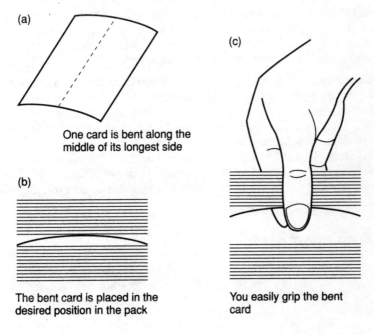

(a)

One card is bent along the middle of its longest side

(b)

The bent card is placed in the desired position in the pack

(c)

You easily grip the bent card

Figure 2.2 How a cheat can ensure the cards are cut in a certain place

Collusion

With poker, the game relies on players not knowing each other's hands. If two or more people are colluding, they can ensure that their best hand is always played. The player with the poorer hand will simply drop out of the betting.

The colluding players will have a set of signals to tell the other player their hand. This can be anything from the positioning of the chips, the lighting of a cigarette or the scratching of an ear.

Combating cheating

If you play in private games, be particularly wary of playing cards with strangers. Obviously you should not play in rooms with mirrors, but be aware that other reflective surfaces can allow a cheat to find out what cards a player has got. With the correct lighting, it is very easy to see what cards are being dealt to players if a table has a highly polished glass or marble surface. You should always, therefore, play on a table covered in felt or with a cloth. Also check the light fittings, some glass lampshades act as excellent mirrors.

Always insist on checking the cards for marks before and after play. Watch the dealer carefully. Does he hold the cards in an unusual way. Someone dealing the second or bottom card is likely to cover the cards with his hands. Always cut the cards by inserting a card not in play like a joker – this gets around the problem of someone bending one of the cards. Keep track of how much money goes into the pot by carefully watching other players when they make their bets. Make sure they add the number of chips required. If you suspect other players of cheating, stop playing.

Burning of cards

Another way to try to combat cheating by the dealer is for several cards to be 'burnt'. The top five cards of a deck are removed and not used in play. However, a skilled technician can still shuffle the cards in such a way that his desired hand will be achieved.

Shuffling and dealing the cards

To ensure the cards are really well mixed, it is best to use a combina-tion of methods for shuffling. Laying the cards face down on the table

and giving them a good mix is a good method of shuffling. This should
be combined with a riffle shuffle. The pack is split into two and your
thumbs are used to riffle the cards so that the two halves are combined (see Figure 2.3).

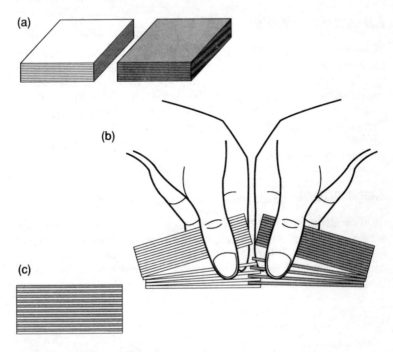

Figure 2.3 The riffle shuffle

The over hand style of shuffling where a number of cards are picked
up from the back of the pack and dropped a few cards at a time to the
front of the pack is most open to abuse as a technician can arrange
the cards into virtually any desired order.

Invite a player to cut the cards. Ensure that none of the cards is
exposed when you deal. Take particular care that the bottom card
cannot be seen by any of the players. Angle the cards down towards
the table when you deal. Take care not to reveal cards that have been
discarded. It is very important that players do not see either the card
on the bottom of the pack or any discarded cards. If a player does see

other cards he can use that information to his advantage. Suppose you see that the card on the bottom of the pack is a king. If you are playing poker and are dealt a pair of queens, you already know that the odds of being beaten by a pair of kings are reduced.

Ensuring fair play

To ensure fair play it is best to play card games in legal casinos. New cards are used each day. They are checked for marks before and after use. If cards do become marked during the course of play, they will be exchanged for new cards. The dealer controls all the betting and will ensure that the players contribute the correct number of chips. Cameras are installed on all the tables to record the action, so if you suspect a player or the dealer of cheating, there is a record of the game which can be studied.

Card counting

Card counting is a technique that allows a player to overcome the casino's advantage in blackjack. However, casinos view this as cheating by the player. If they catch you they will ask you to leave. If you decide to use card-counting techniques you will have to be careful that you are not noticed.

3

THE BASICS OF
BLACKJACK

Blackjack is a card game played with several decks of cards, commonly four or six packs. It is based on the game of 21. Rules may vary in different casinos, so always check them before you start playing. You play only against the dealer, so the other player's hands do not affect your game. To win you need to beat the dealer's hand up to a score not exceeding 21.

Scoring

The cards

All the cards from 2 to 10 inclusive have their face value. The court cards (kings, queens and jacks) have a value of 10. The value of an ace depends on the total score. When an ace is initially dealt, its value is 11. If the player's hand then exceeds a score of 21, the ace then has a value of 1.

Scoring

The value of each card in a hand is added to give the player's score (see Figure 3.1).

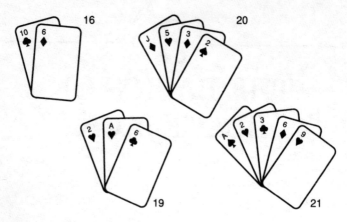

Figure 3.1 Blackjack scores

Blackjack

Blackjack is made by any ace with any card with a value of 10 (see Figure 3.2). It can only be made with the first two cards dealt in a hand. Blackjack beats all other hands, except for a dealer blackjack, when it is a tie or standoff (bets are not lost).

Figure 3.2 Ways of making blackjack

Although the total score of blackjack is 21, it beats a score of 21 made up with other combinations of cards, for example three sevens.

If you have blackjack your bet is immediately paid at odds of 3/2 (one-and-a-half to one) unless the dealer's first card is an ace or worth 10.

In this instance you would have to wait for the outcome of the dealer's hand.

Because only your first two cards can make blackjack, if you receive an ace and a card worth 10 after splitting, you will not have blackjack (see note on splitting on p.16).

How to play

The cards are shuffled by the dealer and cut by the player. They are then placed in a 'shoe' – a special box where cards are placed for dealing. A blank card is inserted roughly one deck from the end to indicate when the dealer should re-shuffle the cards.

After placing their initial bets, each player is dealt two cards face up. Players are not allowed to touch the cards. This ensures that the cards do not become marked. The cards are dealt clockwise starting with the player immediately to the left of the dealer. The dealer also receives two cards. In Great Britain, the dealer initially receives one card only. In the United States, the dealer receives two cards, but one is dealt face down.

Players judge their chances of beating the dealer by the cards they hold and the card shown in the dealer's hand. The cards you have compared to the card in the dealer's hand will determine what you do next. You have several options. You can stand – take no further cards; take more cards to try to improve your score; split your cards into two hands by making an additional bet; or you can double your additional bet.

In Great Britain, you will be asked by the dealer if you want another card, you simply reply yes or no. In the United States the procedure is different. To obtain another card you make a scratching motion on the table. To decline a card, you make a waving motion with your hand.

You can take as many cards as you like to improve your score. If your score exceeds 21, you lose and your cards will be cleared away. You still lose even if the dealer's hand exceeds 21. A tie or standoff only occurs if both scores are equal and do not exceed 21.

Once you are satisfied that you have sufficient cards to beat the dealer's eventual score, you will stand (take no more cards).

After all of the players hands have been dealt with, the dealer will turn his attention to his own hand. If his score is 16 or less, he must take a card. If his score goes above 21 he has lost and all the winning bets are paid. Once he reaches 17 or over he must stand (he can't take any more cards). Any players who have beaten the dealer's score are paid. If you tie with the dealer, your bet is a standoff (not lost).

Examples of outcomes of scores

Dealer's score	Player's score	Outcome
18	19	player wins
17	16	player loses
21	21	standoff (void)
22	20	player wins
19	23	player loses
16	16	standoff (void)
24	22	player loses
21	blackjack	player wins
blackjack	21	player loses

Options

Depending on the initial value of the cards dealt, there are several options available for your next moves.

Doubling

Rules vary as to when you can double, so always check first. In Great Britain, you can make a further bet equal to your initial stake if your first two cards give a score of 9, 10 or 11. Whether or not doubling your bet is a wise move depends on the dealer's score – see the chart on pages 19–20. In the United States you may double your initial bet on any score other than blackjack and take only one more card. Check the chart on pages 19–20 for the best scores to double on.

Splitting

After two cards have been dealt, you have the option of splitting them into two separate hands. An additional bet equal to your initial bet can be made. See the chart on pages 19–20 for the best option. In Great Britain cards with a value of 4, 5 or 10 each are excluded. You would not, in fact, want to split these cards anyway. If two aces are split into two hands, only one extra card can be taken. If you split two aces and then get a 10 value card, this is not blackjack as you can only have black-jack after two cards have been dealt. Instead you have a score of 21.

Odds paid

If both the dealer and the player have the same score, the bet is a standoff (not lost).

Blackjack pays 3/2.

If the player beats the dealer on any other score the odds are 1/1 even.

Insurance pays 2/1.

Insurance

Insurance is an additional bet that can be made if you have blackjack and the dealer's first card is an ace. You make a further bet equal to half your original stake. If the dealer has blackjack, your original bet loses but your insurance bet is paid at odds of 2/1. If the dealer does not have blackjack, you lose the insurance bet, but your original bet is paid at 3/2.

When you take insurance, the outcome is the same whether the dealer has blackjack or not. Your net winnings are even money. Some casinos automatically pay you even money as soon as you take insurance.

Two or more players betting on one box

It is possible to bet on other player's hands by placing a bet in their box. However, you have no control over the hands. The original player makes all the decisions. If the controlling player decides to split, double, or take insurance you do not have to. If hands are split, you have to nominate which hand your bet is on.

Where to place bets

You can bet on as many boxes as you like, up to the table maximum. You can either play yourself or bet on other player's hands.

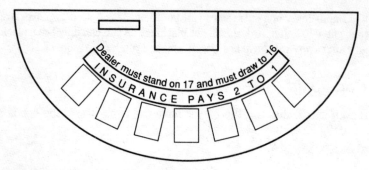

Figure 3.3 The betting layout for blackjack

A single bet – chips placed in the box.

Split bets – chips placed on the line of the box.

Doubled bets – chips placed behind the original stake.

Double split bets – chips placed behind original stakes on the line.

Two bets – chips placed side by side in the box.

Two bets split – chips placed behind each other on the line of the box.

Two bets doubled and split – chips are placed on top of the existing split bets.

It is important to keep track of where you place your bets as, unlike roulette, players use cash chips. It is therefore possible for disputes to arise over which bet belongs to each person. If disputes do arise they are easily resolved by referring to the camera.

4

PLAYING TIPS
FOR BLACKJACK

Practise as much as possible. You can easily recreate the game at home. The chart below shows the best moves to make. Try playing the game at home with the chart beside you, checking each move. With practice you will remember the best options.

The best moves to make in blackjack

C Take a card (draw)   D Double
− Stand   S Split

Player's hand	Dealer's card									
	2	3	4	5	6	7	8	9	10	Ace
8	C	C	C	C	C	C	C	C	C	C
9	C	D	D	D	D	C	C	C	C	C
10	D	D	D	D	D	D	D	D	C	C
11	D	D	D	D	D	D	D	D	D	C
12	C	C	−	−	−	C	C	C	C	C
13	−	−	−	−	−	C	C	C	C	C
14	−	−	−	−	−	C	C	C	C	C
15	−	−	−	−	−	C	C	C	C	C
16	−	−	−	−	−	C	C	C	C	C
Ace 2	C	C	C	C	D	D	C	C	C	C
Ace 3	C	C	C	D	D	C	C	C	C	C
Ace 4	C	C	D	D	D	C	C	C	C	C
Ace 5	C	C	D	D	D	C	C	C	C	C
Ace 6	C	D	D	D	D	C	C	C	C	C

Ace 7	–	–	–	–	–	–	–	C	C	C
Ace 8	–	–	–	–	–	–	–	–	–	–
Ace 9	–	–	–	–	–	–	–	–	–	–
Ace Ace	S	S	S	S	S	S	S	S	S	S
2 2	S	S	S	S	S	S	C	C	C	C
3 3	S	S	S	S	S	S	C	C	C	C
4 4	C	C	C	C	C	C	C	C	C	C
6 6	S	S	S	S	S	C	C	C	C	C
7 7	S	S	S	S	S	S	C	C	C	C
8 8	S	S	S	S	S	S	S	S	S	–
9 9	S	S	S	S	S	–	S	S	–	–
10 10	–	–	–	–	–	–	–	–	–	–

Scoring 16

Lots of players make the mistake of standing on 16 when the dealer has a 7 or higher. The best option is always to take another card. You stand more chance of winning by taking an extra card than you do by standing.

Card counting

Take a pack of cards, shuffle them and split them into two equal piles. Count how many cards of value 10 are in each half. If you do this several times, you will see that the number of tens in each half can vary considerably. This is the basis of most card counting techniques. As a player of blackjack it is to your advantage to know when the remaining cards are rich in tens.

On average the house advantage on blackjack is 5.6 per cent. However, a situation can arise when the house no longer has an advantage. This depends on what cards are left in the shoe. If there are lots of tens left in the shoe, it is in the player's favour. By counting the cards, you can calculate when this situation arises. The most widely used system is to determine when the shoe is rich in tens. This is because dealers must draw extra cards if their score is below 17. However, players can stand on any score. If the deck is rich in tens, the dealer stands more chance of busting. Once this situation arises, you can take advantage by increasing your stakes.

Suppose a dealer's first card is a 6 and the second card is a 10. The dealer has a score of 16, so must take another card. If there are lots of tens in the shoe, the next card is more likely to be a 10 – giving the dealer a score of 26. A player, however, can stand on a score of 16.

Even the dealer's chances of scoring 20 do not place the player at a disadvantage. They each have an equal chance of scoring twenty. A player can also increase his chances of scoring 20 by playing more boxes. If a player bets on all seven boxes, he will have seven chances of scoring 20 compared with only one for the dealer.

Although fewer decks of cards makes the counting easier because the numbers involved are smaller, it can actually be in the player's favour if a greater number of decks are used. If four packs of cards are used and the player realises at the half-way point that they are rich in tens, fewer hands can be played than if six decks are used.

If you decide to use a card counting system, try to find a slow dealer as you have more time to make your calculations. It is also advantageous to sit on the anchor box (the last hand to be dealt). This is because you will see more cards before your hand is dealt. You are in control of the game because you decide what card the dealer gets.

System 1 – keeping track of the tens

The simplest method is to count the tens when they appear. You can judge when you are roughly half-way through the shoe. In four decks there are 64 cards with a value of 10 and in six decks there are 96 cards. So if you are playing with four decks and by the half-way point fewer than 32 cards with a value of 10 have appeared, you know that the remaining cards are rich in tens. You can then increase your bets and/or play more boxes. If the cards are poor in tens, you can decrease your stakes or stop playing.

System 2 – keeping track of the tens and low cards

This system is more accurate because it also takes into account the low value cards which could ruin the previous system if the dealer continually draws low value cards. It involves keeping a running total in your head which requires a high level of concentration.

Starting point for calculating the number of tens	
Number of decks	*Number of cards with a value of 10*
1	16
2	32
3	48
4	64
5	80
6	96

Every time an ace or a 10 is dealt count –1 (minus one). When numbers 2 to 6 are dealt count +1 (plus one). A plus figure means the deck is rich in tens. When this situation arises bets can be increased and/or more boxes played. If there is a minus or low figure either reduce stakes or stop playing.

System 3 – calculating the ratio of tens to other cards

This is more accurate than System 2, but it requires a great deal of mental dexterity and a lot of practice to perfect. Calculations have to be made quickly and accurately.

In a deck of cards there are 16 tens and 38 other cards. The ratio of other cards to tens is $36/16 = 2.25$. When the ratio falls below this level the deck is rich in tens.

Using the system

Count the number of unseen tens and count the number of unseen others. For four decks the starting point for the tens is 64 and the others 144. Deduct one from each total as a relevant card is seen. Divide the unseen others by the unseen tens. If the number is less than 2.25, the deck is rich in tens. Stakes can be increased and or more boxes played when this situation is reached. A number higher than 2.25 is a deck poor in tens. Here you should decrease stakes or stop playing.

Example 1
Unseen tens = 50
Unseen others = 100
Ratio = 100/50 = 2

Here the deck is rich in tens. Bets should be increased.

Example 2
Unseen tens = 40
Unseen others = 120
Ratio = 120/140 = 3

Here the deck is poor in tens. Bets should be reduced.

System 4 – counting fives

An alternative system is to count the fives. When the remaining cards are poor in fives the player has the advantage.

Count the number of unseen fives and the number of unseen others. Divide the number of unseen others by the number of unseen fives. If the ratio is above 13, increase stakes and/or play more boxes. If the ratio is below 13 decrease stakes or stop playing.

The starting points for calculating unseen fives and unseen others		
Number of decks	*Unseen fives*	*Unseen others*
1	4	48
2	8	96
3	12	144
4	16	192
5	20	240
6	24	288

Example 1
Unseen others = 100
Unseen fives = 10
Ratio = 100/10 = > 10

Here the deck is rich in fives, so bets are reduced.

Example 2
Unseen others = 90
Unseen fives = 6
Ratio = 90/6 = > 15

Here the deck is poor in fives, so bets are increased.

Be discreet

For obvious reasons, casinos don't like card counters and do everything in their power to deter them. If they suspect you of card counting, they will make it very difficult for you to continue. They may employ the tactic of distracting your attention. Another way to destroy your chances is to insist that the cards are shuffled more often. Casinos reserve the right to shuffle the cards at any time. If you win lots of money, they may simply ask you to leave. One problem that card counters face is that casinos share information about card counters. So if you get barred from one casino, you could find yourself barred from many other local casinos.

To avoid this situation, you need to attract as little attention as possible. Some players try for a big hit. They play big stakes in an attempt to win as much as possible before being thrown out. This isn't something I would recommend.

On your initial visit to a casino, you will be assessed. If your stakes are small, you will be virtually ignored. If you also play when the casino is at its busiest, you will go unnoticed.

If you play small stakes but then hugely increase your stakes towards the end of a shoe and continually win, you will arouse suspicion. It can therefore help if you develop an erratic betting pattern.

Another method to employ is to work as a team with another player. One person watches a game in progress and counts the cards. A signal alerts a second person that a shoe is rich in tens. The second person comes to the table and starts playing. This way you have avoided betting when the shoe is not in your favour.

You can usually spot when you are under suspicion if the pit boss starts watching your game. However, it is not always obvious as your game can be watched from the camera room. If you think you may have attracted attention, it is best to change to another casino before enough evidence is gathered to throw you out.

Variations on the basic game of blackjack

Some casinos offer additional bets that can be played on blackjack.

Surrender blackjack

This gives you the opportunity to cut your losses when you have a poor hand. After your first two cards have been dealt you have the option to discontinue playing your hand and surrender half of your stake. However, if the dealer has blackjack then you lose all of your stake.

Over/under 13

This is an additional bet. You can bet that your first two cards will be either over or under 13. If they score exactly 13 both bets lose. Odds of even money are paid. If you are using a system for counting tens, you can use this information to your advantage and make this additional bet when the shoe is rich in tens.

Multiple action blackjack

In multiple action blackjack you keep the same hand for three games and the dealer keeps the same up card throughout. A poor hand may mean three losses but a good hand may lead to three wins.

5

PUNTO BANCO

Punto banco is a popular card game based on baccara. All winning bets are paid by the casino but the players take turns to control the bank. On average four decks of cards are used. Paddles are used to move the cards around.

Using a maximum of three cards, the players try to make a score as close as possible to 9.

Tens and court cards (kings, queens, jacks) have a value of 0.

Aces count as 1.

Cards 2 to 9 have their face value.

Scoring

The values of the cards are added to give the score. Cards with a joint total of 10 are given a value of 0.

Examples
7 + 3 = 10 score = 0
8 + 2 = 10 score = 0
6 + 4 = 10 score = 0

Where the cards total more than 10, only the last figure of the total is the score.

Examples
8 + 6 = 14 score = 4
7 + 9 = 16 score = 6

The deal

The cards are shuffled and placed in a shoe. A blank card is inserted about one pack from the end to indicate when the cards should be reshuffled.

Each player makes a bet. The players and the banker each receive two cards. The dealer announces the totals of each hand. If the totals are 8 or 9 that is a natural and no further cards are dealt.

There are set rules that determine whether or not a third card should be dealt.

Chart detailing when an extra card is drawn

Player having

1 2 3 4 5 0	Draws a card
6 7	Stands
8 9	Natural banker cannot draw

Banker having	Draws when giving	Stands when player's third card is:
3	1 2 3 4 5 6 7 9 0	8
4	2 3 4 5 6 7	1 8 9 0
5	4 5 6 7	1 2 3 8 9 0
6	6 7	1 2 3 4 5 8 9 0
7	Stands	
8 9	Natural player cannot draw	

Betting

Each player is playing against the bank and not against one another. The hand with a score closest to 9 wins. The bets are either 'banco' for the bank's hand to win or 'punto' for the player's hand to win. In some casinos it is also possible to bet on a tie.

The layout of tables varies but they are clearly marked with boxes where the banco and the punto bets should be placed (Figure 5.1).

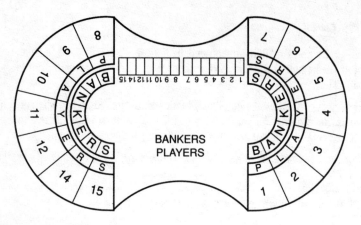

Figure 5.1 Punto banco betting layout

The odds

Punto bets are paid at evens.

Banco bets are paid at 19/20 (evens less 5 per cent commission).

—————— Playing the game ——————

Two cards are alternately dealt to the punto and the banco hands. Where the first two cards total 8 or 9 this is known as a natural and wins outright without the need to take further cards. When there is a tie the hand is replayed. A total of 0 is the worst hand and is known as baccara. The person holding the bank will continue to do so until the banker's hand loses. The bank is then passed to the right, but if the player wishes, it can be passed earlier.

House advantage

The house advantage on punto banco is little more than one per cent with banco bets giving the best value for players. The low house advantage makes punto banco one of the best value games for players. However, there is no skill involved. Players are relying totally on the

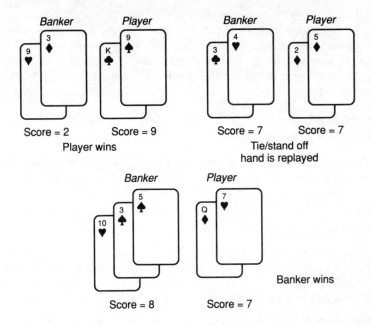

Figure 5.2 Punto banco hands

luck of the deal. All the decisions are made for you according to the rules. As the odds paid are so low it can take a long time for winnings to accumulate.

Staking system

The Martingale system

This system is used for betting on either punto or banco. Stakes are doubled after a loss.

Suppose you wanted to bet on banco. You would wait until punto had won several times. You would then place a bet on banco. If it loses the stake is doubled. If that bet loses the stake is again doubled. The system relies on you always being able to recoup your losses because banco will eventually win.

If you win, you wait until there is another sequence of punto wins and start betting again.

The main problem is the amount of capital that is needed. There may be a run of nine successive punto wins. If your original stake is £1, you would need capital in excess of £1000. However, if banco fails to win on the next hand, your next bet would need to be over £2000 which may be approaching the table maximum, depending on the casino. Once the maximum bet has been reached, you can no longer double up.

The labouchere system

This is a more complicated system for determining your stake. It involves crossing out numbers from the top and bottom of a sequence of numbers to determine what the stake will be.

The numbers 1 to 4 are written down. The first and last numbers in the sequence are added to find the stake.

If you win you cross out the first and last numbers and stake the amount given by adding the new first and last numbers. If you lose you put your last stake at the end of the sequence of numbers and add the first and last numbers to determine your new stake.

When all of the numbers have been crossed out, you write down the numbers 1 to 4 and start again.

The problem with this system is that a losing sequence can soon wipe out both your winnings and your capital.

The reverse labouchere

The systems looked at so far involve risking a lot of capital for small gains. The reverse labouchere differs because it risks a small amount of capital for potentially huge gains.

The same principle is used as the labouchere for determining the stakes, but instead of increasing bets after a loss, they are increased after a win. Once you hit a winning streak, you are effectively playing with the bank's money rather than your own stake.

If you do lose, your losses are minimal. However, if you win the returns can be huge. The table maximums represent the limit of the system. Once the table maximum has been reached, you go back to the minimum bet.

Write the numbers 1 to 4 as follows: 1 2 3 4 .

Add the first and last in the sequence to determine the stake. In this case 5 units. If the bet wins, write the stake at the end of the sequence and again add the first and last to numbers determine the stake.

If you lose, cross out the first and last numbers and add the remaining first and last numbers to find the new stake.

When you have crossed out all of the numbers, you start again with the numbers 1 to 4. Each time you cross out all of the numbers you lose 10 chips.

The table below shows what would happen if the reverse labouchere system was used to bet on both punto and banco. In this sequence punto appears 15 times and banco 6 times. Net winnings = £153.

Example of the reverse labouchere system

Betting on punto

Staking sequence	Stake	Win/lose	Cumulative capital
1234	5	w	5
12345	6	w	11
123456	7	w	18
1234567	8	l	10
23456	8	l	2
345	8	l	−6
4	4	w	−2
44	8	w	6
448	12	w	18
448 12	16	w	34
448 12 16	20	w	54
4 4 8 12 16 20	24	w	78
4 4 8 12 16 20 24	28	w	106
4 4 8 12 16 20 24 28	32	l	74
4 8 12 16 20 24	28	l	46
8 12 16 20	28	w	74
8 12 16 20 28	36	w	110
8 12 16 20 28 36	44	w	154
8 12 16 20 28 36 44	52	l	102
12 16 20 28 36	48	w	150
12 16 20 28 36 48	59	w	210

Betting on banco

Staking sequence	Stake	Win/lose	Cumulative capital
1234	5	l	−5
23	5	l	−10
1234	5	l	−15
23	5	w	−10
235	7	w	−3
2357	9	w	6
23579	11	l	−5
357	10	l	−15
5	5	l	−20
1234	5	l	−25
23	5	l	−30
1234	5	l	−35
23	5	l	−40
1234	5	w	−35
12345	6	w	−29
123456	7	l	−36
2345	7	l	−43
34	7	l	−50
1234	5	w	−45
12345	6	l	−51
234	6	l	−57

6

BACCARA –
CHEMIN DE FER

Baccara – chemin de fer is a combination of the two games baccarat and chemin de fer. It is usually played with six decks of cards although some casinos may use eight.

Instead of betting against the house, you bet against one of the players who is the banker. Players take turns at being the banker with the option of declining the bank.

The aim of the game is to get a score of a maximum of 9 points by adding the values of two or three cards.

Card values

Tens and court cards have a value of 10.

Aces count as 1.

Cards 2 to 9 have their face value.

If a player's total exceeds 10, the number of points in excess of 10 counts as the score. So a total of 16 is a score of 6.

Playing the game

After being shuffled by the dealer and cut by a player, the cards are placed in a shoe. The shoe is passed to the banker – initially the player to the dealer's right. The banker makes a bet of at least the table minimum called the 'bank'. The other players (ponte) can place bets against the bank up to its total amount.

Several situations may arise depending on the amount that other players want to stake. Players make their intentions known by calling out the following:

Banco Solo – By calling out 'banco', one player can place a bet equal to the bank's total. If another player calls banco, the one sitting closest to the right of the banker (prime right) takes precedence over all other players. Players sitting also take precedence over those standing.

Banco avec la table – A player bets half of the bank's total. Other players may bet up to the balance of the bank.

Banco suivi – If any player loses after playing banco solo or banco avec la table, he takes precedence over prime right.

After the bets have been placed, the banker deals four cards face down:

- the first card to the ponte with the highest stake;
- the second to the banker;
- the third to the ponte;
- the fourth to the banker.

The ponte looks at his cards and depending on the score, plays as follows:

0 to 4 asks for a third card;
5 taking a third card is optional;
6 or 7 no action is taken;
8 or 9 the hand is immediately revealed.

A score of 5, 4, 3, 2, 1 or 0 is called baccara.

If the ponte has a score of 8 or 9, the banker cannot take a third card. If, however, the ponte does not have a score of 8 or 9, the banker's decision on whether or not to take a third card is based on the table below.

It is important to take care when dealing or drawing cards as any cards wrongly dealt are given to the player who made the error. This could mean losing when you have a winning hand. Players are allowed to ask the croupier's advice but must follow any advice given.

Action taken by the banker

Banker having	Ponte's third card										Third card not taken
	0	1	2	3	4	5	6	7	8	9	
3	D	D	D	D	D	D	D	D	S	O	D
4	S	S	D	D	D	D	D	D	S	S	D
5	S	S	S	S	O	D	D	D	S	S	D
6	S	S	S	S	S	S	D	D	S	S	S

D: Draw   S: Stay   O: Optional

The banker, banco solo, or any player betting alone against the bank has the option of refusing or declining a card regardless of these rules. But other players must follow them.

The winner is the player with the highest number of points. In the event of a tie, new cards are dealt to each player.

If the banker loses, the bank passes to the right. If the banker wins, he has the option of either keeping or passing on the bank. Players can decline the bank. Anyone accepting it must pay its full value. If no player accepts the bank, it is offered to the highest bidder. When the buyer loses, the bank passes to the player immediately to the right of the previous banker.

When the banker wins, the dealer collects losing bets, deducts 5 per cent commission (*cagnotte*) for the house and adds the remainder to the bank.

If the pontes win, the bets are paid from the bank. No deductions are made from winning ponte bets or drawn games (*en carte*).

Like punto banco there is no skill involved. You are relying on the luck of the deal. All of the decisions are based on the rules. The staking systems described for betting on punto banco can also be applied to this game.

7

THE BASICS OF POKER

What is poker?

Poker is a name given to a huge number of card games. What they have in common is that they are based on the ranking of five card hands. The object of the game is to win the money bet by having the best ranking hand. In order to win you need to beat all of your opponents. The casino supplies the dealer, charging a percentage of the pot (the money bet) for this service. A deduction of around 10 per cent is common.

The main attraction of poker is that it is a game of skill. With many card games you rely totally on the luck of the deal. Poker is entirely different. Even if you have the worst possible hand you can still win the game. This is accomplished with the skilful use of bluffing. You fool the other players into thinking that you have a good hand.

Stakes

The minimum stakes on many poker games are low. The higher the stakes, the better the players, so while you are still learning stick to the cheaper games and gradually work your way up.

The minimum amount of capital you need varies depending on the game. As a rough guide, the capital needed for a game of draw poker is around forty times the minimum stake. With seven card stud approximately fifty times the minimum stake should be sufficient.

Games like 'hold'em' and 'omaha' need around one hundred times the minimum stake. By dividing the amount that you have budgeted by the minimum capital required, you can find the minimum stakes that you can play for.

Get plenty of practice

You need to be able to recognise the value of your hand and where it comes in the ranking immediately. Deal out hands of five cards, identify the poker hands and put them in the correct ranking order. Once you have mastered the ranking you can then start to judge whether or not a hand is worth playing.

Get plenty of practice. Take a pack of cards and deal out dummy hands as if you are playing the game with several players. Practise placing bets as you play. Look at your own hand. Decide whether or not it is worth playing. Then assess your hand against the others. Did you make a good decision? Would any of the other hands have beaten yours? Are you throwing away hands that could easily win? By continuing to do this you will learn the sort of hands that are worthwhile playing and those that are not.

Body language

Poker relies on the other players not knowing your hand. Although the other players cannot see your hand the way that you react to its contents can give them a lot of information.

Players that have complete control over their mannerisms make better poker players. If you can look at your cards and show no facial expressions whatsoever, you make it impossible for the other players to glean any information about your hand.

Keep records

After each game write down the reasons why you won or lost. Analyse the results and learn from your mistakes.

If you lost, try to determine why. Were you staying in when you should have folded? Were you folding with hands that could have won? Were you failing to force other players into folding? Was your body language giving away information?

When you win also try to determine the reasons why. Was it because your strategy was good? Were you just dealt lots of good hands? Did other players make stupid mistakes? Were you picking up on any signs given by the other players?

Periodically analyse your records. They will tell you if you're sticking to your budget and if your betting strategy is effective.

Vary your play

Try not to stick to one style of playing. The most successful poker players are those who are totally unpredictable. If in some hands you play cautiously and in others aggressively you will confuse the opposition. You should aim to vary your betting, the number of cards you take (if playing a draw game), how often you bluff and the signals that you give.

— The standard ranking of hands —

The aim of poker is to win the pot by having the highest ranking hand. A poker hand is made up from five cards. The more difficult a hand is to achieve, the higher its position in the ranking. Figure 7.1 shows how the hands are ranked.

Each type of hand is also ranked according to the values of the cards. The highest value cards are aces and the lowest are twos. The cards are ranked in the following descending order: A,K,Q,J,10,9,8,7,6,5,4,3,2. The suits do not affect the ranking, so if two players both have a royal flush, one with hearts and one with spades, the hands will tie.

The highest ranking hand is a royal flush – A,K,Q,J,10 in the same suit. There are only four ways that this hand can be made, with hearts, diamonds, spades or clubs.

A straight flush is a run of five cards of the same suit in consecutive numerical order.

Four of a kind is four cards of the same numerical value, with any other card.

Figure 7.1 Poker hands ranked from highest to lowest

A full house is three of a kind (three cards of the same value) and a pair (two cards of the same value). Where two players have a full house, the hand with the highest value for the three of a kind wins. So 10,10,10,2,2 would beat 8,8,8,A,A.

A flush is a run of five cards of the same suit in any numerical order.

A straight is five cards of any suit in consecutive numerical order. A,K,Q,J,10 is the highest straight, followed by K,Q,J,10,9.

Three of a kind is three cards of the same numerical value with two cards of different values.

Two pair is two sets of pairs (two cards with the same value) with any other card. *'Aces over eights'* (two aces and two eights) is known as the dead man's hand. It takes its name from the last hand held by the infamous gambler Wild Bill Hickock. In the late 1800s, he was playing poker in a saloon at Deadwood, Dakota. He was sitting with his back to the door when he was shot dead by Jack McCall. His last hand consisted of a pair of aces and a pair of eights.

One pair is two cards of the same value with three other cards of different values. If two players have the same pair, the hand with the highest value other cards wins. A,A,10,7,5 would beat A,A,9,7,5. If all of the cards are of the same value then there is a tie.

Where none of the above hands are held, the winner is the player with the highest card. In a show down a hand containing an Ace would beat one with a King and so on.

The basic game

One deck of 52 cards with the jokers removed is used. Before any cards are dealt, players make an initial bet called an 'ante-bet'. All the bets are placed in the centre of the table.

Each player receives five cards dealt face down. Players look at their cards. A round of betting commences starting with the player to the left of the dealer.

Each player has the option of betting or folding (withdrawing from the game). A player holding a poor hand may decide to fold. If you fold, your cards are returned to the dealer without being revealed to the other players. You lose any ante-bets made.

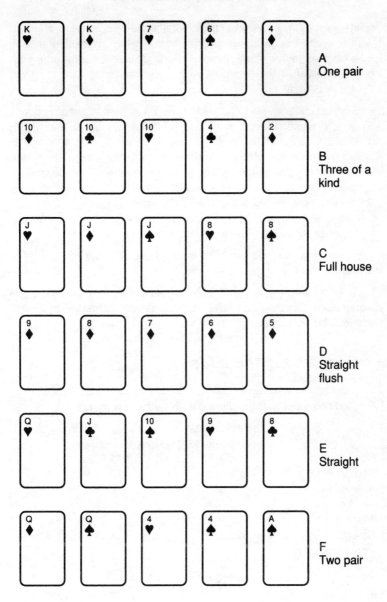

Figure 7.2 Example hands

Some games allow players to check. This usually happens on the first round of betting after the cards have been dealt. Players do not have to participate in the first round of betting, instead they announce 'check'; however, if they want to continue in the game they must bet on their next turn.

The first bet determines how much each player has to bet in order to stay in the game. Players may also raise the bet up to the agreed maximum. To stay in the game you need to bet at least as much as the previous player. Betting continues until either only one player remains or there is a showdown and players reveal their hands. If only one player remains (all the others have folded), he will win the pot. He does not reveal his cards to the other players. If there is a showdown, the player with the highest ranking poker hand wins the pot. In the event of a tie the pot is shared.

In the showdown depicted in Figure 7.2, player D would win as he has the highest ranking hand.

This is poker in its simplest form but it is hardly every played in this manner. Lots of variations have been introduced to make the games more exciting and challenging.

Understanding the odds

The likelihood of being dealt a particular hand in poker		
Hand	*Number of ways it can be made*	*Odds against it being dealt in your first hand*
Royal flush	4	649,739/1
Straight flush	36	72,192/1
Four of a kind	624	4,164/1
Full house	3,744	693/1
Flush	5,108	508/1
Straight	10,200	254/1
Three of a kind	54,912	46/1
Two pairs	123,552	20/1
One pair	1,098,240	1/1

In order to play poker well, a sound understanding of the odds of being dealt particular hands is essential. With games like 'draw poker' you need to know the chances of improving on your hand.

Developing a betting strategy

You need to develop a betting strategy that will maximise your winnings whilst minimising your losses. Your betting strategy also needs to be varied so that the other players can't predict your hand.

Throughout the game you need to pay attention to the way your opponents are playing. Some players may back down after a modest raise, while others may need a huge raise in order to fold. You will be able to spot the players who are staying in the game simply because it is not costing them very much. You may notice that one particular player always folds early on when he has nothing. If he is still there in later rounds of betting, you will know to treat him with caution.

Know when to fold. If your hand isn't good enough to win, withdraw from the game. By continually staying in for one extra round of betting with a hand that is clearly going to get beaten, you lose more money than you need to.

8

FIVE CARD DRAW

Each player receives five cards face down and after an initial round of betting has an opportunity to exchange any card in his hand for new cards from the deck. It is usual to select the cards that are being discarded and to return them to the dealer before new cards are drawn. The table below shows the odds against achieving a particular hand.

Odds against improving hands in draw poker

Hand held	Cards drawn	Desired hand	Odds against achieving hand
3 of a kind	2	any improvement	17/2
3 of a kind + kicker	1	any improvement	11/1
3 of a kind	1	full house	15/1
3 of a kind	1	4 of a kind	46/1
3 of a kind	2	full house	15/1
3 of a kind	2	4 of a kind	23/1
2 pair	1	full house	11/1
2 pair	3	3 of a kind	7.5/1
1 pair	3	full house	97/1
1 pair	3	4 of a kind	359/1
1 pair + kicker	2	any improvement	3/1
1 pair + kicker	2	2 pair using kicker	7.5/1
1 pair + kicker	2	2 pair without kicker	17/1
1 pair + kicker	2	3 of a kind	12/1
1 pair + kicker	2	full house	119/1
1 pair + kicker	2	fours	1080/1
4 card flush	1	pair	3/1

4 card flush	1	flush	4.5/1
4 card open ended	1	straight or flush	2/1
straight flush		straight flush	22.5/1
incomplete straight	1	any improvement	1/1
flush (inside)		pair	3/1
		flush	5/1
		straight	11/1
		straight flush	46/1

— ## What hands should you play? —

There is little point in staying in with anything lower than a high pair. A high pair may be enough to win without any improvement. If, for example, you stay in with a pair of sixes and take three cards in an attempt to get three of a kind, the odds against you achieving your desired hand are 7.5/1. Your opponent may have a pair of jacks and also has the same chance as you of improving. However, if neither of you improves he has already beaten your hand. If you still decide to stay in the game, you need to convince him that you got the desired cards on the draw. Your early bets may have given him no cause for concern. In order to be convincing you will need to make a big raise to force him out. If your bluff fails it may be costly. You may get an indication of the type of hand held from the number of cards that each player exchanges.

If you compare the odds of being dealt a good hand in the first deal to the odds of improving on cards already held, you can see that the odds of improving are much better than the odds of having a good initial hand. So, if in the first deal you have nothing, it is better to withdraw from the game instead of exchanging all five cards. Even exchanging four cards needs something short of a miracle to give you a good hand. You will be betting against players who may already hold good cards and who can also improve by exchanging just one or two.

Holding a pair

If you are holding a pair, you can improve your hand by exchanging up to three cards. However, if you exchange three cards, the other players will be immediately aware that you are likely to have a pair. Anyone with two pair or three of a kind will be confident that he has a better hand.

Instead of drawing three cards, you have the option of keeping a 'kicker'. The kicker will usually be your highest other card. Instead of exchanging three cards, you exchange two. Your chances of improving on your hand are slightly reduced but now the other players will be unsure as to whether you only have a pair or a possible three of a kind.

Do not fall into the pattern of always retaining a kicker when you have a pair as the other players will soon work out your strategy. Vary your play as much as possible so that your opponents are never sure about your hand.

If you decide that the time is right to pull off a bluff, you may decide to take just one card to give an indication of a possible two pair which you are trying to improve to a full house or a flush. In such cases, a big raise would be needed to back up the bluff.

Alternatively you may decide to take no cards. The other players will be aware that you may have been dealt a very good hand, but, again, they cannot be certain. They will be aware of the odds against you getting a high ranking hand with just five cards, and if you have bluffed too often in the past, you are unlikely to get away with another bluff. However, if you are known as a player who rarely bluffs then you may be successful.

Holding three of a kind

You have the choice of exchanging either one or both cards. You have a greater chance of improving to a full house or four of a kind by taking two cards. However, if you always take two cards, you alert the other players to the fact that you are likely to have three of a kind. If, instead, you occasionally exchange one card, keeping a kicker, you will keep the other players guessing.

Holding a full house

It is pointless trying to improve to four of a kind. You already hold a hand which is going to be very difficult for other players to beat. You may decide to raise the stakes to force out other players who may improve on the draw.

Example game

Figure 8.1 shows the hands of four players before and after the draw.

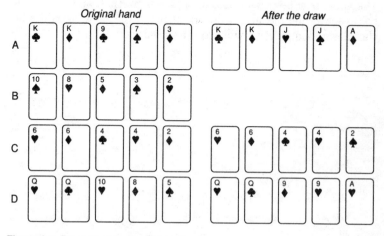

Figure 8.1 Example of five card draw hands

Player A is dealt a good initial hand with a pair of kings. Three cards are drawn. He fails to get three of a kind but gets another pair. The fifth card is an ace. He knows that even if another player has a pair of aces, the fact that he is holding an ace makes it harder for him to achieve three of a kind.

Player B has a poor initial hand so decides to fold.

Player C has two pair. Although the cards are low, he has the opportunity of making a full house by drawing one card. He has seen player A draw three cards, so he knows that A's initial hand is a pair. He fails to improve his hand.

Player D has a high pair of two queens. He is aware that A also initially had a pair. Player C only took one card so he is possibly going for a full house, a flush a straight or is bluffing. D draws three cards and improves to two pair.

Player A raises. Player C decides to fold. He realises that player A may have improved, possibly to three of a kind or two pair. Although player C has two pair, they are low value cards.

Player D knows he has a fairly good hand so he raises player A. He knows two pair with kings or aces could beat him. He holds an ace so knows the chances of player A holding a pair of aces or three aces is reduced.

The game now becomes a test of nerves between A and D. If either backs down then the other will win the pot. If the game continues to a showdown then player A will win the showdown.

9

FIVE CARD STUD

Each player receives five cards from which they make their best five card poker hand. Initially each player is dealt one card face up and one face down. The player with the lowest face up card must make a forced bet. The remaining cards are dealt face up. A round of betting takes place after each card is dealt. The player showing the highest ranking hand is the first to bet in each round.

Here you progressively get more information on which to base your decisions. Once all the cards have been dealt you have a pretty good idea of your opponents' likely hands.

Strategy

If you cannot match or better the highest card showing you should fold. Ideally you should aim for a minimum hand of a high pair.

See Figure 9.1. In the initial deal, player B has the lowest face up card so makes a forced bet. As each card is dealt you get more information about each player's hand. By the fourth card, players A, B, C and D are all showing pairs. Player B has the potential to achieve a straight flush.

By the time the fifth card has been dealt, you can see clearly what the possible hands are. The best hands are A – three of a kind with eights, B – a straight flush, C – three of a kind with sevens, and D – four of a kind with twos or a full house. If each player achieves his best possible hand then player B would win on a showdown.

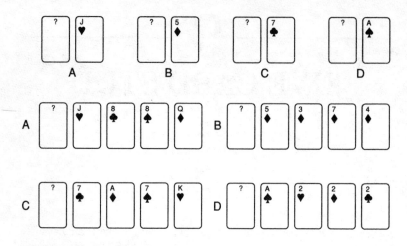

Figure 9.1 Example of five card stud hands

Each player therefore needs to assess their chances of winning against the other hands.

If player A has another 8, he is certain of beating player C. He also knows that if B has any card other than a diamond then his hand is nothing. If player D's hole card is not a 2 or an ace then player A will also beat him. One of the aces is revealed in player C's hand, which gives D less chance of achieving a full house.

Player B knows that he has potentially the best hand. If his hole card is not a diamond then whether or not he wins will depend on how well he can bluff.

If player C has another 7, he will have to decide whether or not the other players are bluffing. Although all the players have the potential for good hands it is unlikely that they will all achieve them. If the other players are all bluffing then he would win a showdown.

If player D has either a 2 or an ace then the only danger is player B. To beat him player B would need to be holding the 6 of diamonds. Any other diamond would only give player B a flush. However, if player D is not holding another 2 or an ace, then he is in danger of being beaten by either A or B – both have the potential for a better three of a kind than his.

10

SEVEN CARD STUD

Seven card stud is one of the most popular forms of poker. Each player receives seven cards. The aim is to make the best possible five card poker hand from the seven cards dealt to you. The player with the best hand wins all the money staked, less the 'rake' (a charge made by a casino for the use of its facilities, usually a percentage of the pot).

Initially three cards are dealt, two face down and one face up. The fourth, fifth and sixth cards are dealt face up and the seventh face down. You therefore have four cards on display to the other players and three cards which are hidden from view.

There is a round of betting after each card has been dealt. The person with the highest ranking poker hand on view is the first to either bet or fold in each round of betting. So someone with three of a kind would be the first to bet if all the other players were showing one pair.

Here you have quite a lot of useful information on which to base your strategy. You may be able to deduce from the other player's four cards on display that your hand has no chance of winning. You can use your knowledge of the odds to calculate your opponents' chance of completing hands that are shown. However, the other players can also deduce the same amount of information from your cards on view.

If your cards on display show the potential for a good hand that could beat the likely hands of all the other players but you do not hold the cards necessary, you have the option to bluff. By continually raising the stakes you may force the other players to fold. The game then becomes a test of nerves. The other players will realise what your potential hand is and will see that you are betting heavily. They will then have to decide whether or not you are bluffing. If you force all the other players to check, you hand is not revealed and they will not know that you were bluffing. If, however, a showdown is reached, your cards will be revealed.

——— **Example hands** ———

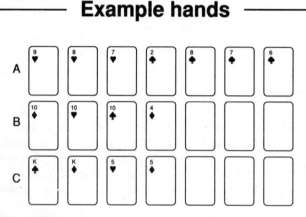

Figure 10.1 Example of seven card stud hands

See figure 10.1. Suppose you are player A. You have two pair. You can immediately see that player B has a better hand with three of a kind. Player C also has two pair which beats your hand, but could have a full house if he has either another king or another five. In the cards that you are showing, you have the 9, 8 and 7 of hearts. Although your hand can't win in a showdown against either A or B, by using a heavy round of betting you could convince them that you have the other two cards necessary to complete the straight flush.

11
HOLD 'EM

Each player receives two cards face down. Five cards are placed face up in the centre of the table. These cards are used by all the players. Each player uses any combination of the two cards in their hand and the five community cards to make the best five card poker hand.

The deal

Initially each player receives their two hidden cards followed by a round of betting. Players often have the opportunity to bet blind (to place a bet before they look at their cards). This helps to increase the pot. Three of the community cards are then dealt, called the 'flop'. Another round of betting follows. A further community card is dealt followed by a round of betting, after which the final community card is dealt.

Since each player's cards are hidden from view, the only indication you have of their possible hands is the manner in which they are betting. In order to make a proper assessment, you really need to see all of the community cards first. Once you have seen these, you are then in a better position to assess the likely hands.

Strategy before the flop

You need to decide whether or not your two cards are worth playing. In general terms it is worthwhile playing any pair, consecutive cards of the same suit, such as 9,8 or 6,5 and fairly high cards of the same suit such as J,9.

Strategy after the flop

You now have a better indication of the possible hands. You can assess your position against all the other possibilities. The community cards may not help you and give other players the possibility of really good hands. If this is the case, then fold now.

If you are still in a fairly good position, you need to force out anyone who can beat you either now or once the other two cards have been dealt.

Nuts

Occasionally a situation may arise where you know that you have the best possible hand (nuts) that can be made using the community cards. There is no way that you can be beaten (see Figure 11.1). Clearly in this situation you want to maximise the pot. Your strategy for betting will need to be based on your knowledge of the players. You need to keep the betting at the right level in order to keep as many of the players betting as possible.

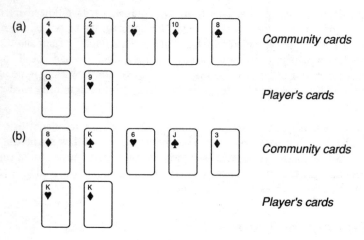

Figure 11.1 'Nuts'

Example hands

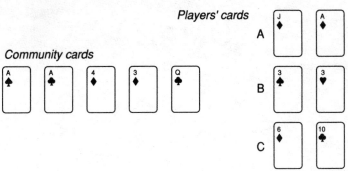

Players' cards

Community cards

Figure 11.2 Example of hold 'em hands

See Figure 11.2. The best possible hand from the community cards is four of a kind, followed by a full house, then three of a kind.

Player A will deduce that he has a good hand with three of a kind. He knows that he has the best possible three of a kind and can only be beaten by a full house and since he holds one of the aces, the chances of anyone holding either two queens, two fours or two threes are low.

However, player B has a full house. He knows that only four of a kind or a full house with queens or fours could beat him.

Player C has nothing and would be wise to fold. Betting would then commence between A and B. It would probably develop into a test of nerves to determine who will fold, or ultimately lead to a showdown which B would win.

12

OMAHA

Each player receives four cards face down. Five cards are placed face up in the centre of the table to be used by all the players. Using any combination of two cards in your hand and three community cards, you make the best five card poker hand.

The game is dealt in a similar way to hold 'em with a flop of three cards. You may also be given the opportunity to bet blind (bet before looking at your cards). What makes the game more complicated is the way in which the five card poker hand is made. When you see the cards you need to give some thought as to what hand you have actually got. At first glance you may seem to have an exceptionally good hand But you need to remember that you can only use two of the cards in your hand (see Figure 12.1).

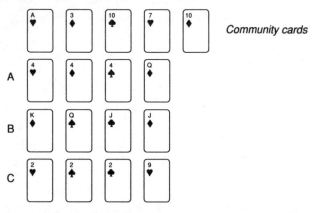

Figure 12.1 Example of omaha hands

By looking at the cards in total, player A can immediately see a full house (three fours and two tens). However, because only two cards can be used from his hand he only has two pair (two tens and two fours).

Player B appears to have a straight (A, K, Q, J, 10) but the hand actually held is two pair (two jacks and two tens).

At first glance player C may appear to have a full house (three twos and two tens). However, he can only use two cards from his hand so only holds two pair (two tens and two twos).

You can get a lot of information from the community cards about the possible hands held by other players.

In Figure 12.1, the possible hands are:

Four of a kind – one player has the other two tens.
A full house – one player has one ten and an ace, seven or three or holds two of the other aces, sevens or threes.
Three of a kind – one of the other tens, or a pair of aces, sevens or threes.
Two pair – a player holds another pair or one ace, seven or two.

Strategy

The strategy is similar to hold 'em in that you really need to see the flop before you can make any decisions. However, a situation can arise when it is wise to fold immediately after you have been dealt your 'hole' cards.

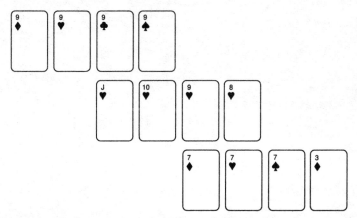

Figure 12.2 Hands to fold on in omaha

Being dealt four of a kind in your hole cards is one of the worst possible situations. You can only use two cards so at best you have a pair with no chance of improving on them. Being dealt three of a kind also gives you a very remote chance that the fourth card will appear in the community cards. The same is true of being dealt four cards to a possible flush, your chances of making the flush are drastically reduced.

The best cards to play with are high pairs or high cards of the same suit (if you hold only two of the same suit) which could lead to a flush.

After the flop, you are in a much better position to judge your chances of winning. You can then assess all of the possibilities and work out your chances of making a good hand. It is at this stage that you need to force out anyone who has the potential to improve their hand into one that could beat yours.

Nuts

As with hold 'em, occasionally a situation may arise where you know that you have the best possible hand (nuts) that can be made using the community cards. There is no way that you can be beaten. Clearly in this situation you want to maximise the pot. Your strategy for betting will need to be based on your knowledge of the players. You need to keep the betting at the right level in order to keep as many of the players betting as possible.

13

CARIBBEAN STUD POKER

The games that we have looked at so far all involve betting against the other players. You have to beat everyone else playing in order to win the pot. Caribbean stud poker differs because it is a banking game. Instead of playing against other players you are playing against the casino which acts as a bank, paying out all winning bets. The casino provides a dealer. In order to win, you have only to beat the dealer's hand. The other players' hands do not affect the outcome of your bets.

The game

The object of the game is to win by having a five card poker hand that ranks higher than the dealer's. Each player makes an ante-bet and is dealt five cards face down. The dealer receives four cards face down and one card face up.

You look at your cards and have the option to play or fold. If you fold your ante-bet is lost. If you decide to play you then make a further bet of twice your ante-bet.

The dealer will then reveal his hand. He must have an ace and a king or higher in order to play his hand. If the player's hand beats the dealer's the ante-bet is paid at evens. See the table overleaf for the odds for the second bet. If the dealer does not have at least an ace and a king then the player is paid even money on the ante-bet and the additional bet is void (not lost). If, however, the dealer's hand beats the player's then both bets are lost.

Payout odds for an additional bet in Caribbean stud poker

One pair or less	1/1 (even)
Two pair	2/1
Three of a kind	3/1
Straight	4/1
Flush	5/1
Full house	7/1
Four of a kind	20/1
Straight flush	50/1
Royal flush	100/1

If the dealer and the player have the same poker hand, the remaining cards are taken into consideration. If all five cards are equal the hand is void (the bet is not lost). Neither the ante-bet or the additional bet are paid. The type of suit makes no difference to the hand.

The disadvantage of this game is that you are relying purely on luck. There is no skill involved. You do not have the opportunity to bluff. In poker games where you are playing for a pot, you are still able to win even with a poor hand but with Caribbean stud poker, if you have a poor hand, you stand little chance of winning.

The minimum odds in this game are evens. In a normal game of poker with, for example, seven players you would have odds of at least 6/1 and quite often a great deal better.

The odds paid for the additional bet are also poor compared to the chances of achieving them. Odds of 100/1 are paid for a royal flush, yet your chances of being dealt one are 649,739/1. The only advantage you have is that you know how much each game is going to cost you.

Caribbean stud poker should only be played for amusement purposes. If you want to win money, you are better off playing games where you are contesting for a pot.

14

PAI GOW POKER

In pai gow poker each player in turn has the option of being banker. The game is a mixture of the Chinese game pai gow and American poker. It is played with one deck of 52 cards, plus one joker. The joker can be used only as an ace, or to complete a straight, a flush, a straight flush, or a royal flush.

The casino provides the dealer. Each player is dealt seven cards. The cards are arranged to make two hands; a two-card hand and a five-card hand. The five-card hand must rank higher than or be equal to the two-card hand (see table of rankings below).

Ranking of hands in pai gow poker

Five-card hand	Two-card hand
Five aces (four aces + joker)	One pair
Royal flush	High card
Straight flush	
Four of a kind	
Full house	
Flush	
Straight	
Three of a kind	
Two pair	
One pair	
High card	

The object of the game is for both of your hands to rank higher than both of your opponent's hands. Your two-card hand must rank higher than your opponent's two-card hand and your five-card hand must rank higher than your opponent's five-card hand.

If one of your hands ranks the same as your opponent's hand, this is a tie (or copy hand). The banker wins all ties. If you win one hand but lose the other, this is a 'push'. In push hands no money is exchanged. Winning hands are paid even money less a 5 per cent commission. Losing hands lose the money bet.

Playing the game

The dealer and each player in turn are all given the opportunity to be banker. You can only be banker if you bet against the dealer the last time he was banker. You need to have sufficient chips to pay the bets should they win.

You arrange your cards into the two hands and place them face down on the table. Once you have put them down, you can no longer touch them. The dealer will turn over his cards and make his hands. Each hand is compared to the dealer's hand. If the player wins one hand and loses the other, the bet is void (a push). If you wrongly set your hand – you lose.

The major disadvantage of this game is that you are relying on the luck of the deal – there is no skill involved. If your cards are poor, there is no opportunity to bluff. The dealer plays his hand if he has the minimum required and does not drop out of the betting.

As with Caribbean stud poker, the odds are also poor compared to playing with a pot.

For an example, see Figure 14.1. Player A has beaten the dealer's five-card hand but has failed to beat the two-card hand. This is a push, the money bet is not lost.

Player B has beaten both hands. His bet is paid at even money less 5 per cent commission.

Player C has failed to beat the dealer's five- and two-card hands. He loses his bet.

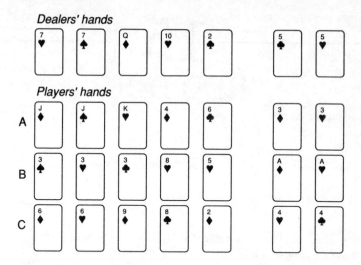

Figure 14.1 Example of pai gow hands

15

RED DOG

Red dog is a simple card game played in United States casinos. The object of the game is simply that players bet that the value of a third card dealt will be between the value of the first two cards dealt.

Card values

Cards 2 to 10 have their face value.
Jacks count as 11.
Queens count as 12.
Kings count as 13.
Aces count as 14.

Playing the game

Two cards are dealt face up. A third card is drawn and placed face up between the first two cards. Players win when the value of the third card drawn is in between the values of the first and second card.

Betting

Bets are placed in the box marked 'bet'. After the first two cards have been dealt, players have the option of making an additional bet up to the value of their original bet. These bets are placed in the box marked 'raise'. This additional bet must be placed before a third card is dealt.

Odds paid

The spread between the first two cards dealt determines the odds paid. The spread is the number of card values between the first two cards drawn.

If the first two cards dealt were a 6 and an 8, the spread would be one, because one card comes between them. If the first two cards dealt were an ace and a 2 the spread would be 11.

Consecutive pair

If the first two cards dealt are of consecutive value, for example, 4 and 5; Q and K; 2 and 3, there is no spread. They are called a consecutive pair. It is not possible to raise this bet.

Pair

If the first two cards dealt are a pair, for example, two sixes or two queens, the bet is void (a tie). This bet cannot be raised.

Three of a kind

This is where the first two cards are a pair and the third card drawn is of equal value.

Odds paid on red dog	
Spread	*Odds paid*
1	5/1
2	4/1
3	2/1
4 to 11	1/1
Consecutive	Tie – no raises
Pair	Tie – no raises
Three of a kind	11/1 – no raises

Red dog should be considered for amusement purposes only. The odds paid are poor compared with your chances of making the point. There is no way that you can influence the outcome and you are dependent entirely on the luck of the draw.

GLOSSARY

Ante – a bet made before any cards are dealt.
Blind bet – a bet that is made without looking at your cards.
Bluff – tricking the other players into thinking that you have a really good hand.
Board – the community cards in games such as hold 'em and omaha.
Bullet – an ace.
Burnt card – a card that is removed from the pack and not used in play. Often several of the top cards will be removed before hands are dealt to combat cheating by the dealer.
Bust – a score over 21 in blackjack.
Button – a plastic marker that is used in casino games to denote an imaginary dealer. This ensures that no player gains an advantage from his position relative to the actual dealer.
Cage – cash point where chips are exchanged for money.
Call – a verbal statement that a player will match the previous bet.
Card counting – a system of counting cards that tips the odds in the player's favour.
Car jockey – someone employed by the casino to park the customers' cars.
Chip – a plastic disc used in place of money for betting.
Community cards – cards which can be used by all the players to make up their best five card poker hand in games such as hold 'em and omaha.
Commission – a charge made by the casino for the use of its facilities, usually a percentage of the pot.
Croupier – dealer.

Dead man's hand – two pair of aces over eights.
Deuce – two.
Door card – in stud poker, your first card that is dealt face up.
Draw – exchanging cards in your hand for cards from the deck.
Flop – the deal where the first three community cards are revealed in hold 'em and omaha.
Flush – five cards of the same suit.
Fold – withdraw from the game.
Fours – four cards of the same value, for example, four queens.
Full house – three cards of the same value with a pair, for example, three aces and two sixes.
Hit – draw another card.
Hole cards – the player's cards that are dealt face down.
Kicker – in draw poker, a card retained to make it more difficult for your opponents to guess your hand.
Marked cards – cards that have been marked in some way so that a cheat can identify their values from looking at the backs of them.
Natural – a score of 8 or 9 in punto banco.
Nuts – a hand in games like hold 'em and omaha which is the best possible hand and one which cannot be beaten by any other player.
Poker face – having complete control over your facial expressions so that you do not give your opponents any clues about your hand.
Pot – the money bet in poker that is placed in the centre of the table.
Rake – in poker, a charge made by the casino for the use of its facilities, usually a percentage of the pot.
River – the last round of betting in poker.
Run – another name for a straight.
Sabot or **Shoe** – a box where cards are placed for dealing.
See – the same as 'call'.
Showdown – when the players reveal their hands in poker.
Stake – the amount of money bet.
Straight – five cards of any suit in consecutive order.
Street – a round of betting. First street is the first round of betting, second street the second and so on.
Stud – a form of poker where some cards are dealt face up.
Sweeten – to add money to the pot, usually in the form of an ante-bet.
Technician – someone who is skilled at manipulating the cards so that he can deal himself a good hand.
Threes – three cards of the same value.
Trips – three cards of the same value.

APPENDIX

Gamblers Anonymous organisations
– in Great Britain, the United States –
and Australia

Great Britain
Gamblers Anonymous
National Service Office
PO Box 88
London
SW10 0EU
Tel: 0171 384 3040

United States
Gamblers Intergroup
PO Box 7
New York
New York
10116
Tel: (212) 265 8600

Australia
Gamblers Anonymous
Head Office
Corner of Dorcas and Montague Street
South Melbourne
Tel: (3) 696 6108

Gamblers Anonymous
PO Box Burwood
Sydney
NSW 2134
Tel: (02) 564 1574

INDEX

ty T E A C H   Y O U R S E L F

How to Win at
POKER

Belinda Levez

This short course will give you a basic knowledge of poker. Belinda Levez is a former casino croupier. In this book she shares her inside knowledge to help you maximise your winnings. All the main games are covered

- five card draw
- five card stud
- seven card stud
- hold'em
- omaha
- caribbean stud poker
- pai gow poker
- poker dice

This book will be a real help both for those who know nothing about poker and for those with some experience who want to learn more and improve the odds for success.

How to Win at
CASINO GAMES

Belinda Levez

This short course will give you a basic knowledge of casino gambling. Belinda Levez is a former casino croupier. In this book she shares her inside knowledge to help you maximise your winnings. All the main games are covered

- roulette
- blackjack
- punto banco
- dice/craps
- poker
- two up

This book will be a real help both for those who know nothing about gambling and for those with some experience who want to learn more and improve the odds for success.

Other related titles

TEACH YOURSELF

How to Win at
HORSE RACING

Belinda Levez

This short course will give you a basic knowledge of betting on horse racing. Belinda Levez is a former betting shop manager. In this book she shares her inside knowledge to help you maximise your winnings. All the main areas of betting are covered

- off-course betting
- tote betting
- bookmaking
- selecting winners
- getting the best price
- betting strategies
- calculating winnings
- ready reckoner

This book will be a real help both for those who know nothing about betting and for those with some experience who want to learn more and improve the odds for success.

Other related titles

ty **TEACH YOURSELF**

SUCCESSFUL GAMBLING

Belinda Levez

Teach Yourself Successful Gambling is a complete guide to gambling and betting.

Belinda Levez is a former betting shop manager and casino croupier. In this book she shares her inside knowledge, to help you maximise your winnings. All the main areas of gambling are covered

- racing
- sports
- casino games
- lotteries
- bingo
- pools
- slot machines

This book will be a real help both for those who know nothing about gambling and betting and for those with some experience who want to learn more and improve the odds for success.